BEING BAPTISED
The Handbook to Believer's Baptism

AF215997

Stephen Gaukroger with Simon Fox

Faithbuilders Publishing UK

BEING BAPTISED by Stephen Gaukroger.

© Copyright Stephen Gaukroger 1993 (with Simon Fox), 2003, 2019

ISBN: 9781912120413

Faithbuilders Publishing

12 Dukes Court, Bognor Road, Chichester, PO19 8FX, UK

www.faithbuilderspublishing.co.uk

British Library Cataloguing-in-Publication Data. A catalogue record for this book is available from the British Library

All scripture quotations are taken from the Contemporary English Version (CEV) published by The Bible Societies/ HarperCollins Publishers © 1991, 1995 American Bible Society.

Illustrations by Rowin Agarao

Cover Design by Faithbuilders Publishing.

Printed and bound in Great Britain

To Susie

About the author

Stephen Gaukroger, born in Sheffield, was converted, baptised and called to the pastoral ministry while attending Carey Baptist church in Preston, Lancashire. Following training at Spurgeon's College, he spent a year on the staff of First Baptist Church, Dallas, Texas.

Currently he is Senior Minister at Gold Hill Baptist Church, on of the largest churches in England. He is a prolific author with a popular style. Many of his 19 books have been widely translated.

Stephen is regraded as one of the most significant leaders of his generation in the UK. He has a clear grasp of postmodern culture and addresses its challenges with an unquestioned commitment to Scripture.

He regards mission/evangelism as a key priority for the Church, both locally and nationally, and it is this reality which drives his leadership. Until recently Stephen was a leader of Spring Harvest, widely recognised as the most influential Christian teaching event of the last 25 years. He was president of the Baptist Union of Great Britain from 1994–95, and now serves on the council of Spurgeon's College, chairs the European Board of the Luis Palau Evangelistic Association and also chairs the Council of Reference of the European branch of Jews for Jesus.

He is married to Janet, who is very involved with worship and with Christian work among under fives, and they have three children.

Contents

1

Come on in – the water's lovely!

I have baptised hundreds of people – and it never becomes dull or repetitive! Perhaps you think that once a minister has been in the water twenty or thirty times, baptism loses its appeal – but that's not so. I still find baptism fascinating and exciting, because God is always there in the pool, making himself known in many different ways.

I have seen all sorts of people get baptised. Some were teenagers, others were mature adults. One woman was ninety-three years old! Some who were elderly or sick have hobbled with help into the pool others have literally run down into it. One person weighed just six and a half stone. I felt I could have baptised her with one finger! Another weighed sixteen stone. One man was six feet six inches tall. I have been involved in the baptisms of people of many different ethnic, social and educational backgrounds. All these people had come to faith in Christ and wanted to be baptised as an expression of that faith.

A life-changing event

I can clearly recall so many of them. There was John, who had been rescued from a life of drunkenness; there was Paul, a respectable businessman, apparently with very little to say sorry to God for. There was the sprightly older lady who had been a lifelong member of the Salvation Army and wanted to make a public declaration of her love for Jesus. There was the young mother who had never had anything to do with the Church, but who had suddenly encountered God. Tears of joy streamed down her face as she gave her testimony at her baptism.

For many people baptism is a very moving experience: it can be an exciting and life-changing event. I'll let just four people I've baptised tell their own stories. But first one person will tell what convinced him to be baptised.

WANG: 'I love him and want to be in union with him'

'I came from Beijing in China to study – but after little more than a year in the UK I found something far more valuable than my MBA!

'Back in 1976 I survived a great earthquake in Thangshan, China. In 1989 I escaped the fires and guns of Tiananmen Square when the government cracked down on the democracy movement. Neither of these experiences made me a new man! However, my life was transformed in the 1990s when I met God. 'In China I was a businessman for a state-run firm and had an easy life with my wife and our lovely daughter. I underestimated the difficulties in coming to England and pursuing academic study after not studying for more than 15 years. I had language difficulties and lacked professional knowledge. Also, my health was bad – problems with my blood pressure and with my spinal column. In the first four months I lost 25 kilos in weight and was debating whether to return home. But a friend invited me to church and I became interested.

'If you had told me I would be interested in God I would have said, "Ridiculous!" But I felt moved by the friendship of the people at the church. They helped me overcome one obstacle after another. With their advice and prayerful support I gradually gave up worrying. They taught me to control my anger, not to judge others, to care for others unselfishly.

'So I decided to believe in God and receive him into my life. In fact, I found he was the source of all life. There were difficulties, but I began to grow closer to God. I was confident that I had God in my heart and I was cared for by my brothers and sisters.

'Amazingly, I passed all my exams! I knew that the most important factor in that success was God's mighty power. He was the source of my strength and of my peace of mind. I knew that without God I was nothing at all.

'Before I return to Beijing, I want to be baptised to show that I will follow my God through my whole life. I love him and want to be in union with him. I know there are many obstacles or evils in the future. God will help me overcome them.'

SUSAN: 'I felt I was being received by Jesus'

'I had been a Christian for six years. God had challenged and changed me a great deal, and yet I had a growing desire to be completely released from my past and to receive new life and freedom. I wanted to feel clean. I was holding on to a lot of old hurts, disappointments and patterns of behaviour because they made me feel safe. I wanted to give them to the Lord and to be relieved of the burden.

'One day another Christian told me that they felt God was saying I should be baptised. For a few months I prayed about this, wanting to know if it really was from the Lord. Seeing other people get baptised, meeting people who witnessed to the difference which baptism had made to them and, most important of all, hearing from God, convinced me that I too should get baptised. Once I had made that decision, I became very aware of God's hand upon my life. On several occasions I had a feeling of being held and protected by him.

'During the months leading up to baptism, God gave me time to repent, to turn away from my old patterns of behaviour and to turn to him with a new faith. I also had to forgive other people and myself for things which had happened in the past.

'On the day of my baptism, during the prayer time before the service, I had a real sense of being filled spiritually, of being in God's holy presence. As I entered the pool I felt some last-minute doubts about what I was doing, but knew there was no way out – I could only go forward! The two ministers in the water welcomed me with open arms. This was very symbolic to me – I felt I was being received by Jesus.

'Since my baptism my life has been challenging, but I have also had greater spiritual strength and resources. I have felt an eagerness to pray, at anytime and anywhere! I have had a new ability to witness to others about Jesus.

'However, I still feel that I haven't given myself over to God wholly yet: I have a desire to give back to him the 'new me' he has redeemed and healed. God is continuing to change me – this is the hardest part. But I believe that the Lord has a purpose for me and that he's equipping me for it through this tough training. I am aware, too, that baptism is only a part of my walk with Christ – it is not an ultimate goal in itself.

'The most important thing since my baptism is the feeling which I now have of having been cleansed. The relief was wonderful, and the release was tremendous!'

HEATHER: 'I feel completely different'

Heather wrote this letter to me the day after she was baptised: 'I am so excited that I don't know what to write! I feel completely different – not at all like me. I have no recollection of sleeping before 3 am. I just lay there in the most glorious state of bliss.

'Today I still feel completely overawed and not really here. I feel so full of God that I'm ready to burst. I seem to be walking round with a permanent grin, feeling shaky with a strange yet peaceful agitation about me.

'Steve – what is this? Has the Lord been so good as to baptise me in his Spirit? Is this why my world is so different today?

'Thank you, thank you for yesterday. It was the most wonderful experience of my life… I shall never forget it – any of it. I know I will "come down to earth" eventually and must continue to pray for more and more of the Lord in my life. I do long to get out there and be of real service to my Lord, to give my life to seeking and doing his will.

'Thank you for the most precious gift anyone could be given…'

Some time later Heather wrote me another letter:

'… I wrote to you four months ago to tell you of the amazing things I was experiencing after my baptism… four months on things are still amazing! This was not a stupendous "quick-then-over" experience but an ongoing one – God is refilling me with his Spirit almost daily; my prayer life is in a completely new dimension; praying in tongues has become so natural and lovely; I'm so aware of the Lord's presence so often now.

'Initially I was unsure if the Lord had used my baptism to baptise me in his Spirit – I couldn't really believe it had happened to me. Now I cannot doubt it. I can feel him influencing me in all I do, gently bringing me back when I mess things up; he is no longer just a part of my life but all of it. I'm never more content than when I'm in conversation with him…'

MARTIN: 'an amazing power inside me'

Heather's husband Martin was baptised at the same time. He too was blessed by God through baptism. This is his letter:

'I thought you would be interested to hear of the wonderful and exciting things God has been doing in me since my baptism. 'I have to confess that before the service I was mildly apprehensive that although I was being baptised in water I would miss out on a touch from the Holy Spirit, although I knew you would pray that I would experience this. I couldn't imagine anything like that happening to me – I couldn't actually imagine what other people meant by it, anyway.

During the service, however, I had a picture from God. I had never known what these kinds of pictures were like, but I believe it was from God. As you were praying for one of the other baptism candidates I saw a sky completely covered with grey clouds; then the clouds parted and the sunlight streamed through. As I said, I didn't know much about pictures, but I felt a little excited about this. Then my concentration returned to the service.

'The following morning in school, in the little quiet time I snatch before the pupils and other staff arrive, I had another picture. This time it was an image of an empty cross with flames burning out of the top of the upright... Ever since then I have felt an amazing power inside me, growing and fading repeatedly but getting stronger each time. Sometimes the feeling is so strong that I feel I will burst, and it seems to me that if I were just to point my finger at something a miracle would happen.

'Twice this week I have woken up in the early hours and have been filled with this feeling. I have stayed awake, lying in bed and contemplating the wonder of Jesus and praising him and praying to him in my mind. During these experiences I have also felt an extraordinary peace. I wasn't in the least bit bothered that I would feel absolutely shattered the following day! I just felt blissful.

'This has been a tremendously exciting time for my wife and me. I thought the baptism service was fantastic, but I had no idea that all this was going to follow! I had no preconceived ideas about what a baptism in the Holy Spirit was like, but I am sure that is what I received. I thank you for praying for it and I thank the Lord for giving it.

'I am waiting for God to tell me what he wants me to do for him. At least I now know that he can and will make himself heard. God is so wonderful!'

BRIAN: '... feeling of oneness with God'

Brian writes:

'Baptism seemed great for those who felt they needed it. But, looking at all the people my wife Jenny and I grew up with – all good Christians and none of them baptised – we felt that we didn't need it when we became members of our local Baptist church. After all, we were growing in the Lord and fully committed to him.

'I was less reluctant about baptism than my wife. Her prayer had often been, "I'll do anything you want, as long as you don't ask me to be baptised."

'For some time we drifted along. I even asked God to reveal his will for us on the subject, although I also made the terms clear:

I was happy to conform in principle, but I wanted to wait until my wife felt equally comfortable about being baptised. It seemed like a safe bet to me! But still there was no answer from God and no apparent change of heart from Jenny.

'One Monday morning as I was driving to work, I was praying. I often do this when driving. I was simply asking God for guidance as to what more I should do for him. Something else I often do when driving alone is to listen to tapes of sermons which I had missed, and I did that this morning. Instant answers to prayer had always been things which other people had: they had not really been a part of my own experience. But that morning the Lord spoke clearly to me through the tape: "Of course you should be baptised – my Word tells you so!"

'And so the decision was made. My feet probably did touch the ground during that day, but I didn't notice! But that evening I came down to earth with a bump: I knew I had to tell my wife that I was not going to wait any longer to be baptised. I phoned her and told her that I was going to write to our pastor and ask to be baptised. To my amazement she replied, "Tell him I want to be baptised as well."

'This was the confirmation I needed that God had truly spoken to me. During the weeks leading up to our baptisms we were more relaxed and peaceful in God than ever before, because we knew that we were at last being obedient to his Word. We were both afraid of giving our testimonies, of looking like complete idiots, and even of the water itself, but these fears were overshadowed by our feeling of oneness with God. I can honestly say that the decision I made on that Monday morning as I was driving to work was one of the best and most important I have ever made.'

Read on!

I know many other people who could tell similarly meaningful stories about their baptisms. Some people's experience of baptism is spectacular, while for others the event has a more ordinary quality. I had a very 'fireworks-free' baptism. Spectacular or ordinary, other people's descriptions of their baptisms should encourage us to push forward in our exploration of believer's baptism and cause us to ask questions like:

Why should a Christian be baptised? What is baptism really all about? Why does it mean so much to those who experience it? Why do so many people find that it changes their lives?

For answers to these questions, read on!

To recap

• Baptism is important – it can seriously change your life!

2

Tackling the groundwork

The fact that you're reading this book at all probably means that you're interested in or considering baptism. Perhaps some of your friends have been baptised recently: you've seen how important and exciting it was for them, and so you're thinking that you would like to be baptised too.

But wait a minute! Before you get baptised, you need to do a little bit of groundwork. Baptism is meant only for people who are committed to Christ, so you need to make sure that you really are a Christian.

Are you a Christian?

Only God can make you a Christian. Jesus has already done everything necessary for you to be saved. All you need to do is respond to what he has done.

Jesus said, 'You must be born again' (John 3:3). In other words, to become a Christian you have to make a completely new start in your life. But how can you do this?

There are two key steps in becoming a Christian: **repentance and faith**. Without those two things – whatever your background or lifestyle – you're not a Christian according to the definition the Bible gives us.

The first step is **repentance**. This means saying sorry to God for all the wrong things you've done and for failing to meet his standards, and meaning it enough to do something about it.

Repentance is not just remorse – 'I wish I hadn't done it, because now I've been caught and I'm in a lot of trouble!' True repentance is saying to God, 'I'm really sorry. I don't want to live my life my way any more – I want to live it your way.' The word 'repentance' literally means 'turning around' – turning away from the old life and cowards God. Anyone who becomes a Christian, sets off in a new direction.

To do so no more is the truest repentance.

Martin Luther

The second step is **faith**. This means putting your trust in Jesus to sort out the wrong things in your life; it means inviting him to come into your life to change you and be real to you. Faith needs to be genuine and personal. You need to be able to say, 'I have come to know this Jesus because I have asked him into my life.'

This is a very important foundational truth. God has no grandchildren – only children. Your parents may be Christians, but that in itself does not make you a Christian. You may go to church regularly. You may have Christian friends. But, again, these things do not necessarily mean that you are a Christian. Only a personal friendship and relationship with Jesus makes someone a Christian.

It's very important that we really understand that we can't rely on the faith of our parents, our friends or anybody else. Becoming a Christian is a decision we each have to come to **personally**.

Faith essentially means taking someone at their word.

David Watson

It's really useful to check all this out with someone in church leadership. Talk to your house group leader, your elder, your minister, or a Christian friend. Make sure that you understand exactly what's involved in becoming a Christian.

Becoming a Christian

You can experience the new life which Jesus gives as you:

• recognise that you need help – All of us have sinned and fallen short of God's glory (Romans 3:23).

• turn your back on everything you know to be wrong – 'Turn back to God! Be baptised in the name of Jesus Christ, so that your sins will be forgiven' (Peter to crowds of unbelievers in Acts 2:38).

• trust Jesus to put things right – Christ carried the burden of our sins. He was nailed to the cross, so that we would stop sinning and start living right (1 Peter 2:24).

• invite Jesus to be in charge of your life –… some people accepted him and put their faith in him. So he gave them the right to be the children of God (John 1:12).

You can pray a prayer which goes something like this:

> Dear God, I am sorry for all the wrong things I have said and done and thought. I would like to make a new start. Jesus, thank you that you died on the cross and rose from the dead for me. I ask you to come into my life. I hand my life over to your control. Help me to love you and follow you – now and always. Amen.

Rainy days in April

I want to emphasise that what I am trying to do here is to challenge possible complacency, not to encourage doubt. I'm asking you to make sure that you really are a Christian and not just to assume that you are.

However, what I don't want to do is disturb the faith of those people who really are Christians, who have truly given their lives to Christ, but who have internal emotional doubts. There are many people who are in this situation. Indeed, it's probably true that at one time or another most Christians experience doubts about whether or not they really are converted.

We need to remember that becoming a Christian is not primarily to do with the emotions. Rather, it is a decision of the will. That's why it's important to talk to someone in leadership about this, because sometimes they can give you their reassurance that you are a Christian when you can't feel God's reassurance. They can tell you, 'Yes, we've seen evidence of God working in your life; we know that you genuinely do want to follow Christ' even though you may not have a very strong feeling that you are a Christian.

It's like being a member of a cricket team. There may be days when you're out on the pitch and you score a quick 40 runs for your club and you feel fantastic! You walk back to the pavilion feeling as if you're a great cricketer. But then there are also the wet, cold April days when you hate the whole game. You're out on the first ball, you trudge back to the pavilion and sit around feeling fed up.

On those April days you are no less a member of the cricket team than you are on the sunny days when you play well. The fact is that you have signed up and you are a member, and that's the end of the matter. Whether you always feel like a member or not is irrelevant.

If you have joined Christ's 'team' by asking him to come into your life as your Lord and Saviour, then you are a member. You are a Christian and a member of Christ's Church. Whether or not you feel that you're a Christian is, in the final analysis, not important. You need to focus on the facts rather than on your emotions.

There are a lot of rainy, cold April days in the Christian life, because we are affected by things like mood swings and adverse circumstances. In this fast-changing world we are on the receiving end of a lot of shocks.

For example, if you are a teenager your life is changing rapidly. You're going through all the problems of puberty and adolescence. You're facing changes in your body and emotions which are bewildering. It's hard to feel secure about your faith when these things are happening to you.

If you're about to leave university or college, you have to make big decisions about your future career. You're anxious about getting on the career ladder and wondering if gloomy forecasts about economic downturns will prove correct. Even if you have a job, you may not feel very secure in it. You're wondering if it's time to move on and add to that portfolio of skills you're always hearing people talk about.

Another big decision you may be facing is housing. Perhaps you're thinking about buying your own home. But can you really afford it? If house prices are soaring, is this the right time? If they're stagnant, should you rush in and take advantage? Would it be more sensible to rent, or is it foolish to spend so much on monthly outgoings with no return?

Then there's the whole question of relationships. Should you live with your girlfriend or boyfriend before marriage? If you marry, should you have children, and if so, when? What are the implications of bringing children into today's world? Being a parent is a big responsibility. Do you think you can cope with it? If you are in your forties or fifties you may have to contend with the emotional turmoil of a mid-life crisis. Or perhaps you have been made redundant, and getting another job at your age is proving to be difficult. If you are in your sixties or older, you may be facing the frightening uncertainties of retirement, the disappointment of a poor pension, failing health, maybe bereavement.

Life can be tough in the high-speed third millennium! We are frequently pressured and sometimes tormented! We face upheavals and crises. Everything conspires to make us feel insecure. True, Christians often talk about feeling secure because they know Jesus as their Lord and Saviour. It's perfectly right to preach on the Christian's eternal security in Christ – but this is not linked necessarily to feelings of security. In reality, many Christians feel unsure and insecure about their salvation. This does not mean that they are not Christians. We should not place too much emphasis on feelings, because they can be altered so swiftly and so drastically.

However, to be baptised you must be 'born again'. This does not necessarily mean that you know the precise day or hour when you became a Christian. But it does mean that you know you have made a conscious decision to follow Jesus. If that is not true of you, you ought not to be considering baptism. On the other hand, if you have made a clear commitment to Christ but you feel insecure about it and relatively little seems to have happened and there's no dramatic sense of God in your life, that is not a reason not to be baptised. If you have genuinely given your life to Christ, go ahead and enjoy all the benefits and blessings of baptism!

To recap

• Before getting baptised, make sure you really are a Christian.

• Being born again involves repentance and faith, based on what Jesus has done.

• Becoming a Christian is not primarily about feelings. If you have genuinely given your life to Jesus, you are a Christian, even if you don't feel 'saved '.

3

Nuts and bolts of baptism

What do we mean by believer's baptism? We are not necessarily talking about adult baptism, but about the baptism of those who are committed to following Jesus and who want to be obedient by being baptised. So these people could be teenagers or possibly even children, but they could not be babies, because babies are incapable of such commitment. If you are under eighteen, most churches will want to get your parents' agreement before baptising you.

Sometimes I have been asked to baptise a child but have been unwilling to do so because I have not been absolutely convinced that the child has really become a Christian. Can he or she express, either by the spoken word or in writing, what it means to be a Christian? I don't mean they need to express it in an adult sense, but in a way which shows that a real encounter with Christ has taken place. In some cases I've come across, the child has only a superficial understanding about Jesus and the gospel, and the real motivation behind the request for baptism may be parental pressure. Sometimes there is even a superstitious element to such pressure – parents want to ensure that if their child dies, he or she will go to heaven.

This book is not intended to defend the argument for believer's baptism. I have no wish to get involved in that huge debate here! It is true that nationally and internationally there is more and more support for believer's baptism, and less for infant baptism. Of course, that is not an indication of whether or not infant baptism is true or right – many true and right things are out of favour in popular culture. For example, in our society marriage is losing ground against the practice of living together – yet I am entirely in favour of marriage!

Baptism should be only for those who have made a conscious decision to accept Jesus as Lord and Saviour. However, that leaves us with the question of people with learning difficulties or intellectual disability. They may be incapable of understanding much doctrine. We need to remember that it's quite alright for someone to express their faith in Christ in the simplest of terms. I have baptised some people who have had a very limited understanding of the gospel. But, as far as they were capable, their decision to follow the Lord Jesus Christ was real and valid. So we should remember not to stress the intellectual element of personal faith to the detriment of those who are simply not capable of making such an informed decision.

What form should baptism take?

So the most important thing that should be said about baptism is that it is for those who have made a clear decision to follow Christ. In Acts 18:8 we read that 'all the people who had faith in the Lord were baptised'. An issue of secondary importance is what form of baptism should be used – that is, how it should physically be done.

There have been disagreements about this down the centuries. One of the earliest Christian writings, the Didache, says that people should be baptised three times in running water – each immersion for one of the three Persons of the Trinity.

> Baptise as follows: After first explaining all these points, baptise in the name of the Father, and of the Son, and of the Holy Spirit, in running water. But if you have no running water, baptise in other water; and if you cannot in cold, then in warm.
>
> The Didache

PASTOR TIM BELIEVED IN TOTAL IMMERSION...

These days there are three recognisable forms of baptism in water:

• sprinkling (usually on the forehead),

• effusion (pouring water on the head and the hands) and

• total immersion.

Any of these forms could legitimately be used for believer's baptism. For example, I once baptised a woman in her nineties who was infirm, confined to a wheelchair and unable to leave her own home. So I baptised her in her home by effusion. That was a perfectly valid and genuine baptism.

However, the Bible clearly points to full immersion as the normal form of baptism. There are several reasons for taking this view. First, full immersion is the form which best symbolises the New Testament's teaching on baptism. The visual imagery used about baptism implies full immersion. Paul says, 'When we were baptised, we died and were buried with Christ.

We were baptised, so that we would live a new life, as Christ was raised to life by the glory of God the Father' (Romans 6:4). The picture is of drowning or dying (going under the water) and being raised to new life (coming up out of the water). It's just as clear in Colossians 2:12 – 'And when you were baptised, it was the same as being buried with Christ. Then you were raised to life because you had faith in the power of God, who raised Christ from death.' Full immersion symbolises burial with Christ far more vividly than sprinkling or effusion.

One of the ideas behind baptism is washing or cleansing. This is a very strong biblical image. In Mark 1:4 we read that 'John the Baptist appeared in the desert and told everyone, "Turn back to God and be baptised! Then your sins will be forgiven".' So baptism was linked with cleansing and forgiveness – it was, if you like, taking a bath with spiritual significance. So this aspect of the meaning of baptism also suggests that the most appropriate form of baptism is total immersion.

Secondly, full immersion is the form which best conforms to what we know of baptism as practised in New Testament times. For example, we have the baptisms John the Baptist performed in the River Jordan. In John 3:23 we read that he was at a place 'where there was a lot of water, and people were coming there for John to baptise them'. Why did the believers go to the Jordan to be baptised? If full immersion was not the best form of baptism, they could presumably have been baptised by sprinkling or effusion elsewhere.

And then there is the Ethiopian official's baptism in Acts 8:38. The text reads, 'Then they both went down into the water, and Philip baptised him.' Why did they go into the water if Philip merely needed to pour a little water on the man's head? All the relevant New Testament passages suggest that a large volume of water was required for baptism.

Thirdly, the Greek word 'baptize' originally meant 'to submerge' or 'to immerse' or 'to drench'. It was used with reference to the dyeing of cloth, in which process the whole of the piece of cloth would be submerged in the dye. There would have been no point in merely sprinkling dye on a piece of cloth!

To recap:

• Believer's baptism is the baptism of people who are committed to following Jesus. These people can be adults or teenagers or children.

• There are three possible forms of baptism in water: sprinkling, effusion and total immersion. Any of these forms could legitimately be used for believer's baptism, but the Bible points to full immersion as the norm.

4

Whys and wherefores

People often tell me why they don't want to be baptised or why they think they don't need to be baptised. I've heard them all!

• It's inconvenient.

• I'm frightened of going under the water.

• My parents weren't baptised.

• I don't want to look foolish in front of the whole church.

• I'm nervous about speaking in public.

• It's not necessary for someone who's been a Christian for many years.

• What will it give me that I haven't already got?

Of course, there is some substance to each of these reasons. None of us wants to look foolish in front of family and friends – although if we do go ahead with baptism, we are likely to gain their respect for having the courage of our convictions. Fear of water is a genuine difficulty for some – but God can give us the strength to overcome such fear. Talking with other Christians who have had similar fears can be a great help.

However, none of these reasons carries much weight when compared with the reasons why we should be baptised. Let's examine them.

A biblical command

The first and most important reason why we should be baptised is that the New Testament commands it. As he ascended into heaven, Jesus ordered the apostles, 'Go to the people of all nations and make them my disciples. Baptise them in the name of the Father, the Son, and the Holy Spirit' (Matthew 28:19). Peter said, 'Turn back to God! Be baptised in the name of Jesus Christ, so that your sins will be forgiven' (Acts 2:38). If you believe that the Bible is God's Word, you have no option but to take it seriously and do what it says.

The witness of the New Testament

Secondly, the general witness of the New Testament is that there was no such thing as an unbaptised believer. Apart from the thief who was crucified next to Jesus (who, for obvious reasons, was not baptised), all the believers depicted in the New Testament were baptised. Baptism was part and parcel of their faith.

The story of the Ethiopian official, chief treasurer in the royal court, told in Acts 8, is relevant once again. It's a remarkable story. Philip goes to this man and sits with him in his chariot. The man is reading Isaiah 53:7,8 and asks Philip, 'Tell me, was the prophet talking about himself or about someone else?' Philip replies that Isaiah was speaking about Jesus, and he goes on to tell the official the gospel. The man is evidently convinced by what Philip tells him, and almost immediately says, 'Look, here is some water. Why can't I be baptised?'

It's astonishing to us that he could progress so swiftly from reading Isaiah to hearing the gospel to being baptised! After all, suppose that while out driving one day I pick up a hitchhiker.

He isn't a Christian, but he happens to be reading a copy of the New Testament, and he mentions this to me. Now, baptism would not be one of the first things about Christianity that I would mention to him. I would ask him about his life and get to know him; I would talk about the Bible and the gospel message – I would mention baptism only later on.

However, the fact that the Ethiopian asked to be baptised suggests that Philip mentioned baptism to him at an early stage in his witnessing. From this we may conclude that baptism was an essential part of the gospel message for him and for the rest of the early Church.

In fact, baptism crops up continuously in the New Testament. For example, in 1 Corinthians 12 and 14, where Paul talks about spiritual gifts and the life of the Body of Christ, he says, 'God's Spirit baptised each of us and made us part of the Body of Christ' (12:13). The idea of an unbaptised Christian would have been unthinkable to the first-century Church.

The example of Jesus

And yet many people today think of baptism as an 'optional extra'. This is particularly true of people who have grown up in Christian homes or joined a church practising believer's baptism after being in churches which don't practice it. They often assume that baptism is for new believers.

So thirdly, we must take into account the example of Jesus. He was the perfect, sinless Son of God, so he, more than anyone else, could say that he didn't need baptism – and yet he was baptised (Matthew 3:13–17). If even our Lord and Saviour felt it necessary to be baptised, then it seems somewhat presumptuous of us to assume that we don't need to be baptised!

These three reasons for being baptised that we've considered are directly biblical. We will now look at two other reasons which are more personal.

An encounter with God

First, baptism is an opportunity for an encounter with God.

Throughout the New Testament baptism in water and baptism in the Holy Spirit are linked. For example, Jesus was baptised in the Holy Spirit immediately after being baptised in water by John the Baptist: 'As soon as he (Jesus) came out of the water, the sky opened, and he saw the Spirit of God coming down on him like a dove. Then a voice from heaven said, "This is my own dear Son, and I am pleased with him'" (Matthew 3:16,17).

On the other hand, the household of Cornelius were baptised in the Spirit before being baptised in water (Acts 10:44–48).

There are those who teach that the two baptisms are in fact the same thing and happen at the same time; there are those who believe that one should precede the other. But the important thing is that the act of obedience which is water baptism does seem to be linked with a spiritual encounter with God. Both the New Testament accounts and the experience of con- temporary Christians demonstrate this. I know of many people whose lives have been transformed by baptism, whose testimony is, 'I met God in the pool'.

When considering getting baptised, many people are prompted by the thought, 'Yes, I do need more power in my walk with God; I do need to be equipped to be the person God wants me to be.' In a sense this is a 'selfish' motivation for getting baptised. But it's a biblical motivation none the less – a desire to know and experience more of God.

A question of obedience

The second of the more personal reasons for baptism is perhaps more 'selfless' than the first: it is basically a question of lordship and obedience. Who is in charge of my life? If God is, then I will do what he wants me to do – even if that is not necessarily what I want to do. Yes, it certainly can be embarrassing to take a 'bath' in public! But if I believe that God wants me to do it, I will do it. If I am going to claim that Jesus is my lord, I cannot pick and choose what he will be lord of and what he won't be lord of: he must be lord of all my life.

Therefore, since Jesus and the New Testament command that I should be baptised, I need to respond in obedience to this command.

Obedience is all over the gospels. The pliability of an obedient heart must be complete from the set of our wills right on through to our actions.

Catherine Marshall

This question of obedience is of great importance today. We live in a society which increasingly challenges authority structures. When told what to do, more and more often people are inclined to disobey. There is a widespread spirit of independence which says, 'Why should I do what you tell me to do?'

We see evidence of this all around us. There are problems with discipline in schools, where teachers are denied traditional punishments and pupils refuse to conform. In families, many parents don't know how to control their children. The young are often unwilling to accept authority and that means flouting the law. Breaking into cars and joyriding; vandalism; theft of mobile phones with threats of violence; shoplifting – such crimes committed by young offenders are reaching epidemic proportions.

But this lawlessness is not confined to the younger generation. If you drive on the motorway at the top legal speed of 70 miles per hour, yours is often the slowest vehicle on the road! Many drivers simply ignore speed limits – unless, of course, they're approaching a speed camera!

Large-scale financial fraud is another sign of lawlessness in our society. For example, during boom times many stock market buyers and dealers grow rich and powerful – and some of them believe that they have a right to maintain this even if it means cheating on their customers or abandoning their integrity with 'insider dealing' or corrupt accounting practices.

Many people today behave as if obeying the law is something only others have to do. If they do obey the law, they do so only to avoid punishment, not because they think the law ought to be obeyed. Obedience is very unfashionable, and very counter-cultural in a society which highly prizes the right of an individual and demeans the common good..

Without wishing to be too sentimental about the past, it's true that in previous generations concepts such as obedience, duty and loyalty were very important. People felt a duty to stay with their marriage partners; they went through bad patches, but they remained faithful to each other. Many people went to church out of a sense of duty, even when it was inconvenient or difficult.

Today this sense of loyalty and duty has to a large extent disappeared. Marriage isn't seen as a lifelong commitment. Many Christians stay in the local church only if it's fun. If the going gets tough, they go elsewhere. Indeed, some Christians, having discovered that the Christian life is not a bed of roses, abandon their commitment to Jesus altogether.

But Christians are meant to be different from the secular society in which we live: we are called to be obedient and loyal to God. And baptism is one way of declaring that God is in charge and that we are determined to obey him. Baptism strikes a crippling blow at the selfishness which is at the heart of our fallen human nature. This is one of the most crucial reasons why baptism is important.

By being baptised we are saying, 'This is obviously what you want, Lord. By going through with this I am affirming that you have the right to exercise authority in my life. I submit to you. '

The issue is not whether the idea of baptism appeals to us, but whether it is right. Very few of us like going to the dentist! But we go because we need to – in the long term it is the right thing to do. We don't enjoy having inoculations against diseases when we go abroad; we do it because it is the wise and right thing to do. We refrain from robbing a bank not because we don 't like the idea of being a quarter of a million pounds better off but because robbery is a crime and a sin! Having said that, most people find that being baptised is a much more joyful experience than going to the dentist!

Every revelation of God is a demand, and the way to knowledge of God is by obedience.

William Temple

Giving your life to Christ is not a casual decision to be taken lightly; it's not about having a nice feeling inside. When we become Christians, we enlist in God's army: he becomes our Supreme Commander and we give up the right to run our own lives. We may not always like or understand the Commander's orders, but if the army is to be effective in fighting the enemy, all the troops must obey him. In fact, in the spiritual front line, obedience may save the Christian soldier's life.

JANET: 'It's not much to ask.'

Janet's story is an example of someone getting baptised because of a desire to obey God and to show gratitude to him. She and her husband Rod had attended different churches over some years, but when they moved to a new area they started going to a Baptist church. Rod had for some time been thinking about being baptised as a believer, and eventually he took this step. He was followed by his daughter and then by his son.

'However', says Janet, 'I still held out against it, since my confirmation in the Anglican Church meant a great deal to me… One other major thing was that I did not like going into water, and to have to go under the water backwards was just not on!'

Some time later Rod and Janet were involved in a road accident. Their car was badly damaged, but they were unhurt. It could easily have been a different story.

'That night,' says Janet, 'I couldn't sleep, so I spent some time reading the Bible at my bedside. I opened it at random and read one of the accounts of the crucifixion of our Lord. It was as if he was saying to me, "I went through all this pain for you. I saved you from all the pain of a nasty accident. Now, will you be baptised? It's not much to ask." At breakfast the following morning I told the family what God had said to me and that I would be baptised.

'My baptism service took place a couple of months later. It was recorded, and on the video tape you can see that my hands reached out to hold on to something as I was lowered into the water! But getting baptised was just a little thing I did compared with what Jesus did for us all on the cross. Thank you, Jesus.'

To recap:

Why get baptised? Because…

• The New Testament commands it. There was no such thing as an unbaptised believer in New Testament times.

• Jesus himself was baptised. If even Jesus, the sinless Son of God, felt it necessary to be baptised, then we certainly ought to be baptised as well!

• Baptism is an opportunity for an encounter with God.

• Being baptised is an act of obedience; when I recognise that if God is in charge of my life, then I will do what he wants me to do.

5

Getting ready for baptism

If you were going to have a job interview soon, you would prepare thoroughly for it. You would think about what to say and how to say it. You would give some thought to what you should wear.

At your baptism you will be having an 'interview' with God – encountering the most important Person in the Universe! So careful preparation is essential.

Confession

As baptism is a sign of the washing away of sin (Acts 22:16), one of the major things you need to give attention to during the weeks (and even months) before the event is the whole area of confession. Being right with God is something we should always be concerned about.

David prayed, 'Look deep into my heart, God, and find out everything I am thinking. Don't let me follow evil ways, but lead me in the way that time has proved true' (Psalm 139:23,24). In another psalm he pleads, 'Please have pity on me. You are always merciful! Please wipe away my sins. Wash me clean from all of my sin and guilt. Create pure thoughts in me and make me faithful again' (Psalm 51:1,2,10). He wrote this after he had slept with Bathsheba and arranged the death of her husband. David had committed two great sins, and as a result there was a huge spiritual blockage in his life. Until he was genuinely repentant about his sin, his life came to a standstill.

It's so important to have a thorough clear-out of your life before you get baptised. You need to take time to say sorry to God for your past sins – for the wrong attitudes you have held, the wrong actions you have done and the people you have hurt. Ask God to remove the devil from any part of your life where you think he may have a foothold. Take time to examine your own soul. That sounds old-fashioned, but it is as important now as it ever was. In our busy, fast-moving world this is something we tend to neglect.

If you don't take time to prepare for your baptism, its deep significance may elude you. There is a tendency sometimes to minimise confession as an important aspect of discipleship. People think, 'Jesus accepts me just as I am, so let's just get on with Christian living.' It's true that he accepts us just as we are, but that is from his perspective. From our perspective, we need to allow him to make us holy. However, I would like to emphasise that we should let God convict us of our sins. We should not get involved in a dredging operation, searching our subconscious for things to say sorry for. God will bring into our minds the things we need to repent of, and he will do this as and when he wants to. There is absolutely no need for us to make things up! What we do need to do is to make ourselves submissive to his purposes.

As God shows you the things in your life which you need to repent of, you might find it helpful to make a list of them. Then, once you have asked for God's forgiveness for all those sins, you can tear up the list and throw it away! This act can powerfully symbolise the fact that when God forgives us our sins, he also forgets them; and it reminds us that we should forget them too.

Think through the basics

It is important to think through the basics of the faith. Consider and replay in your mind the way in which you came to Jesus, and thank him for that. Make sure you understand the fundamentals of the faith such as assurance of salvation, the Bible, prayer, the Church, guidance and so on. If you're not sure about anything, ask your minister or pastor for some guidance or for one or two good Christian books to read. You might consider doing a discipleship course. Some churches offer special courses for people who are preparing for baptism. This is an ideal time to cover this sort of ground, even if you've been a Christian for 20 years or more.

I remember seeing a television interview years ago in which Bill Shankley, one of the all-time great football managers, was asked about the secret of the Liverpool team's success under his leadership. He replied that he didn't make his team do anything complicated or out of the ordinary, that he just taught them to 'do the simple things well'. My advice to you is, 'Make sure that you are doing the simple things in your walk with God well'.

Prayer and Bible reading

Take time each day in the weeks preceding your baptism to focus your thoughts on it. Make sure you are daily in touch with God through prayer and Bible reading. These two spiritual disciplines, which we are liable to neglect in our busy lives, are always important, and especially so at this crucial time in your life.

Prayer is a shield to the soul, a sacrifice to God, and a scourge to Satan.

John Bunyan

At the end of the book you'll find some guidelines about Bible reading and a special seven-day Bible reading plan to help you during the week before your baptism.

Fasting

It may well be a good idea at this time to practise fasting. This can be a tremendously helpful spiritual discipline. Particularly in the Old Testament, it expresses repentance and a serious desire to deal with sin. Since one aspect of the meaning of baptism is a washing away of sin, fasting is very appropriate as part of baptism preparation. It acts as a physical reminder of the seriousness of baptism: it focuses the mind on spiritual issues.

Personally, I find fasting a remarkably difficult discipline, but also an amazingly effective one. It makes me aware of my over-dependence on physical things, as I become hungry very quickly. It forces me to reckon again with the supernatural and to reflect on how easy it is for my fleshly desires and concerns to force God out of my mind.

You might consider fasting for one day a week for several weeks leading up to baptism. This need not necessarily be a 24–hour fast; try doing it from dawn to dusk.

Keeping a journal

It is worthwhile keeping a spiritual journal during the period before your baptism. In it you can note down the Scripture verses through which God has spoken to you, your prayer requests and how they have been answered, and your own reflections on your baptism and what it means for you.

Commission

There was a commissioning component in the baptism of Jesus. God was authorising him to go out and fulfill the tasks set for him. After being baptised Jesus went out into the wilderness and was tested by Satan, and then began his ministry. His baptism launched him into the work for God which he had to do on earth. And the same principle applies to you. During the time before your baptism you need to think about your whole life and the task or tasks which God wants you to do. You need to be aware that your baptism is a public declaration of the lordship of Christ over your life, and you need to be asking yourself where this might lead you. What does he want you to do? How does he want you to do it? Where will he send you? Getting baptised in itself is an act of obedience, and it implies further acts of obedience. For example, are you willing to be a witness for Jesus in your place of work? Are you willing to serve him on the mission field in another part of the world?

A 'spiritual director'

It can be very helpful indeed if during this preparatory period you have a 'spiritual director' – that is, someone you can go to for help and encouragement, who can review all the aspects of your life with you. A mentor like this can look you in the eye and say, 'How is it with your soul?' He or she is someone you allow the right to question you about your faith.

This is another neglected spiritual discipline today! We don 't like other people having that kind of authority over us. Having a spiritual director challenges self – always a good thing – and it allows God to open another window into our being, so that we can see ourselves from a different perspective. At the very least we see ourselves as another person sees us, and at best we will see ourselves as God sees us.

Wise friends make you wise, but you hurt yourself by going around with fools.

Proverbs 13:20

There are plenty of biblical examples of people's eyes being opened by God through another person. In Acts 9, Ananias is sent by God to restore Saul's sight. God could have done it without using Ananias, but he chose to do it through him. I think that story is a lovely picture of the way God often uses other people to open our eyes to ourselves, to our world and to others.

So it can be especially helpful during our preparation for baptism to have some kind of 'confessor' figure. We make ourselves accountable to a trusted friend or spiritual leader who knows us well and who will pray with us and for us. This person is not to make decisions for us, but is to help us to be honest with ourselves and with God.

To recap:

In the weeks and months before your baptism:

• Open yourself up to the Holy Spirit so that he can convict you of your sins. Repent of the sins he shows you, and so get right with God.

• Think through the basics of the faith. Join a discipleship course. Make sure you are doing the simple things well.

• Be in touch with God through prayer and Bible reading.

• Fast, perhaps for a day each week.

• Keep a spiritual journal.

• Think about your whole life and the task or tasks which God wants you to do.

• Meet regularly with a 'spiritual director'.

Of course, you need not stop doing these things once you have been baptised! If you continue with them they will help you to grow and mature as a Christian.

6

More practical matters

Now for some more mundane but equally essential areas of preparation for the Big Day!

Preparing your testimony

You may well be asked by your church leaders to tell everyone at the baptism service how you became a Christian. It is important to plan your testimony well. Unfortunately, testimonies are often very poorly prepared!

There are four basic elements you need to include:

• What your life was like before you became a Christian.

• How you heard the gospel and became aware of the Christian faith.

• The process by which you became a Christian.

• How you came to the point of wanting to be baptised.

Of course, this is just a general guideline: don't feel that you have to follow this format rigidly.

God did not save you to be a sensation. He saved you to be a servant.

John Hunter

I advise candidates for baptism to write down everything that occurs to them under the four headings above, and then go through it all very carefully to exclude any trivia and to ensure that the main points are made clearly. There will probably be several other people getting baptised at the service, so you will have only two or three minutes to give your testimony. It's a good idea to read it to a friend before the day, so that they can tell you whether or not it makes sense and whether you ought to change it in any way. ·

Of course, you don't have to use a written testimony at the service at all, but it's best to write it down in the event (not unlikely!) you get nervous on the day: you will then be able to read it out without having to worry about what you're going to say!

Make sure that you don't embarrass people in the congregation. For example, don't say, 'I grew up in an ungodly home' if your parents are present at the service! It's important to think about the impact of your testimony on the people who will hear it. Remember that by saying how you became a Christian you can greatly encourage those people who helped you along the way to commitment to Jesus.

Try to get the balance of your testimony right. Don't talk for two and a half minutes about how sinful you used to be and then spend just thirty seconds on how you came to Christ.

The style is important too. I have heard so many testimonies which make the non-Christian life – going to parties every night or whatever – sound far more interesting and exciting than becoming a Christian, which sounds incredibly dull by comparison! Your testimony needs to honestly depict your non-Christian life: it should not paint an excessively sinful picture just for dramatic effect. The simple truth is far more effective. The main point you are trying to get across is that you love Jesus and have decided to follow him for the rest of your life. Don't lose sight of this!

So long as our personal testimony exalts the glory of Christ as Saviour rather than our character either before or after conversion, it will be helpful.

Robert Belton

It is probably better not to have an evangelistic appeal at the end of your testimony, unless this can be done very naturally.

Making an appeal is the minister's job; not yours! Your task is simply to state the facts about how you became a Christian, to say what a difference it has made in your life and how you have come to the point of being baptised.

When you actually give your testimony at the service, remember to speak slowly and clearly and to take deep breaths so that your voice will have plenty of volume. Look up at the audience as you speak – otherwise your voice won't carry and no one will hear the testimony you have prepared so carefully.

Promises

Sometimes, in addition to giving a testimony, or instead of it, the baptism candidate may be asked to make certain promises, perhaps along the following lines:

Leader: Do you believe in one God, Father, Son and Holy Spirit? Candidate: I do.

Leader: In obedience to the call of our risen Lord Jesus Christ,

do you repent of your sins and come to be baptised?

Candidate: I do.

Leader: With the help of the Holy Spirit, do you offer your life in service to God wherever he may call you to go?

Candidate: I do.

Leader: Then come and be baptised.

(From Patterns and Prayers for Christian Worship: Baptist Union and Oxford University Press)

Choosing your song

At many churches the people getting baptised are allowed to choose a hymn or song or scripture reading to accompany their baptism. Your baptism is a very special occasion for you, so choose carefully. Is there a Bible passage which helped you to become a Christian? Is there a song which is of great personal significance to you?

Recording the day

You may be either so nervous or so taken up with the immediacy of your baptism that you won't be able to take a great deal of it in, so watching or listening to a recording of it at your leisure afterwards can help you to appreciate all the details of it more fully. In years to come that recording will remind you of the event and will refresh your sense of commitment and calling. It will also be encouraging to hear your own testimony again. You might want to show it to those who couldn't or wouldn't come to the church.

A video camera is more suitable than a conventional camera, as flashes can be obtrusive in a baptism service. Careful planning will avoid distraction for you, for the others being baptised, and for the congregation. Sort out the details beforehand – where the person recording the video will stand, where the microphones will be and so on. It's important that the video should not get in the way of things. It is best if the person operating the video stays in one place throughout the service. Make sure that your arrangements for recording the service are approved by the leaders who will be conducting it.

Alternatively, you might be satisfied with an audio recording. If your church has a PA system, you should be able to get a recording done on that, perhaps on CD or MP3.

What to wear

People used to be given gowns to wear at their baptisms, but these days they are usually baptised in their own clothes. Whatever you wear, it should be lightweight. Heavy clothes become even heavier when they're waterlogged.

Women ought not to wear anything which will become transparent when wet! It may be better to wear trousers or jeans, as a skirt (unless the hem is weighted) will float up around a woman's waist when she is in the water. It may be a good idea for women to wear their swimsuits underneath their normal clothes – this solves any embarrassing problems with underwear.

If you wear a t-shirt at your baptism, it shouldn't be brightly coloured or one with a striking slogan which will draw attention away from the serious purpose of the service! The congregation's attention should be focused on Christ and the gospel – not on what you are wearing.

It's better not to wear socks, as you may slip in them once they are wet. Step carefully down into the pool barefoot. Remember to bring a complete change of clothes with you.

On the day

Arrive at the church half an hour before the service begins, not five minutes before. Allow yourself plenty of time to get ready – you don't want to have to rush around at the last minute, trying to find a room to change in! Check that you know where you're supposed to be sitting and when in the service your baptism will be happening. Sorting out these little details can help to make the service less stressful and more enjoyable.

Remember to take your watch off before your baptism – even if it's a waterproof one. And if you wear glasses, don't forget to remove them, too. Make sure that your pockets are empty – you don't want to discover some soggy paper tissues in them after your baptism! These things are obvious, of course, but they are just the sort of things you may forget in the excitement of the day.

In the pool

If you are frightened of water – and a surprising number of people are – one idea is to go to the local swimming pool with a friend and have a 'practice' baptism. Sometimes I advise people who don't like water to wear their swimsuits underneath their clothes; often that will make them feel a bit more secure.

Be warned – sometimes the water is cold! On a few occasions I have had to baptise people when the church's water heating system wasn't working at all, and as a result the water in the pool was near to freezing point!

If you are being baptised by total immersion, which is generally done backwards, remember to keep your legs straight on the way down and to bend them on the way up. If you bend your legs when you're on the way down it's hard for the minister to get you completely under the water; if you keep your legs straight on the way up it's hard for him to get you out of it! Take a short breath as you start to go backwards. You'll only be held under the water for a few seconds, so be relaxed about it.

Afterwards

Don 't forget to invite someone to be your 'towel holder', so that when you come up out of the water they can wrap a towel around you. This person could be your 'spiritual director' or a friend who has helped you in your Christian life.

It's a good idea to bring two large towels. You might also like to bring a hairdryer. You won't want to look like a drowned rat when you go and talk to your family and friends after the service!

To recap:

• Prepare your testimony well.

• If you are going to make promises at the service, think and pray about them beforehand.

• Choose your song or Bible reading carefully.

• If you're going to record the service, plan it well.

• Think about what to wear, and when to be at the church.

• Take a deep breath and keep your legs straight as you go under the water and bend your legs as you surface.

• Ask someone to be your 'towel holder'.

7

Making the most of the day

There are various ways you can make your baptism a really effective evangelistic tool.

Your testimony

It is important to prepare your testimony with the non-Christian guests at the service in mind. You don't need to preach at them, but explain simply what has happened to you. Make sure that as far as possible your testimony is free of jargon – that it communicates clearly to ordinary people and not just to a 'religious' audience. Avoid words which non-Christians won't understand, such as 'salvation', 'sanctification', 'justification', and so on.

Don't present your testimony in a 'conspiratorial' sharing style: 'You all know that Jesus has come into my life, and you all know how wonderful it is…' Tell your story as if nobody present understands what it means to become a Christian.

Remember that your guests will be people who know you well, so you had better be honest about yourself!

Chapter 6 also gives some practical advice on preparing your testimony.

Leaflets to give away

It is a good idea to ask your minister if a table can be set up in the church, so that guests who want to know more about Christianity can take away some free evangelistic booklets – perhaps Journey into Life or something similar. It is best if there is no one manning the table, so that people don't feel shy about going to it. If there is an evangelistic appeal in the service, there should be something for those who respond to it – a Gospel or New Testament, perhaps.

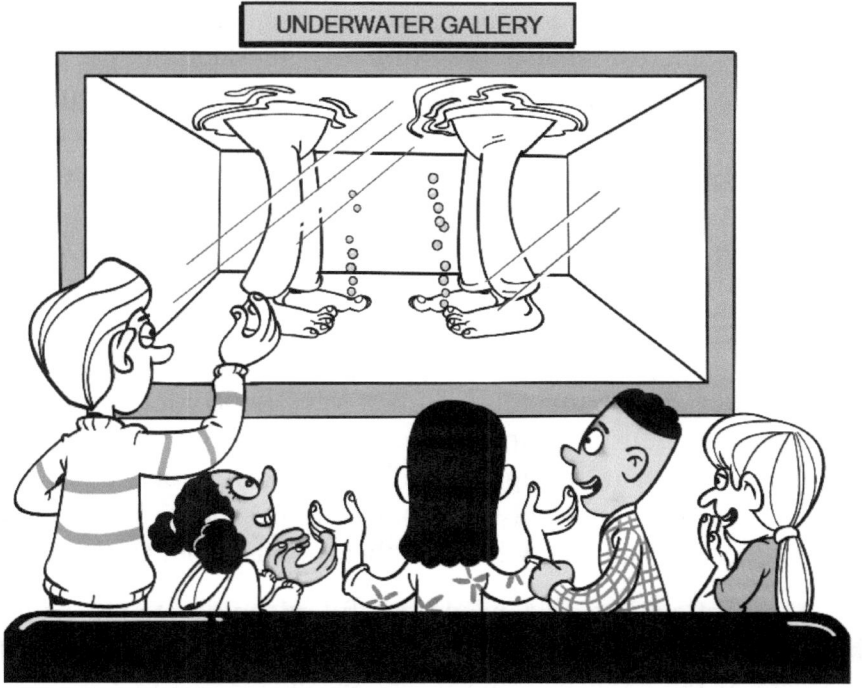

Follow-up

This may be the first time some of your guests have been to church at all, or for years. Perhaps some of your Christian friends could sit with them so that they feel a little less out of place. It's a good idea if the minister can announce when the next evangelistic or baptism service will be; perhaps he could give details of when and where the house groups meet – with the clear message that any of the guests are welcome. So if people are too embarrassed to say there and then, 'Yes, I'd like to know more about how to become a Christian,' they can at least turn up at a future meeting which sounds interesting.

Many evangelistic endeavours in our churches fall down because we assume that we're going to get conversions with just one shot, whereas it often takes several shots. We have something to learn from the marketing strategy which used to be used by some companies. If you ever replied to one of their offers, you were destined to receive literature from them for the next three hundred years! They knew that the fact that you had showed even just a little interest in their products meant that you were a much better marketing opportunity than Joe Public, who had never shown any interest whatsoever. Similarly, the fact that the guests have come to the baptism service, even if just out of politeness or friendship to you, shows that they have at least a faint interest in Christianity. In evangelism the concept of 'repeat customers' is a crucial one.

A reception

Many people lay on a reception of some kind for their family and friends after their baptism. This is a very good idea, especially from an evangelistic point of view. Some of your guests will never have been to a baptism before, and over food and drink they will unwind and feel freer to ask what baptism is all about, or any questions they may have on their minds about Christianity.

A reception like this needs careful planning. Some people have attractive wedding-style invitations printed. Tell your guests the date of the baptism some weeks in advance so that they can make travel arrangements. If some of your guests are travelling a long way it might also be a good idea to lay on a meal for them before the baptism.

In Jesus' ministry, personal invitation was the usual evangelistic method. A general invitation to your baptism in the local press is unlikely to have much effect! The personal approach to evangelism is always better. If you invite your friends, they will probably come, not because they are particularly interested in baptism but because they are interested in you as a person. Effectively you are saying to your family and friends, 'My baptism matters very much to me. Please will you come and share it?'

Publicity

Publicity after the event is well worth thinking about. It's a good idea to write an article about your baptism for your church magazine – people will be interested to know what it meant to you. Alternatively, you could write it as a letter to your local newspaper. A good photograph of the occasion will make the letter more publishable. Local papers are often interested in reports of baptisms. You might even consider inviting a reporter to the service. A newspaper will be especially interested if you are a well-known person in the community. Local radio is another possibility. The media are interested in stories about things which are happening to local people, and that is just what baptism is.

A story to tell

In the weeks to come you will have an interesting story to tell to your colleagues, neighbours and non-Christian friends. 'You'll never guess what I did on Sunday. I had a bath in public!' Needless to say, that doesn't happen very often, and people will want to know about your baptism. You will have a superb opportunity to speak about your faith.

To recap:

To make the most of your baptism as an opportunity for evangelism:

- Prepare your testimony with non-Christian guests in mind.

- Ask for free evangelistic literature to be made available.

- Ask for some kind of follow-up to the service to be arranged.

- Consider laying on an after-service reception for your family and friends.

- Tell the local media about the baptismal service.

- In the weeks after your baptism you will have an interesting story to tell. Use it to witness to others about Jesus.

8

Encountering God in baptism

For many years churches practising believer's baptism were guilty of being all form and no reality. They didn't expect God to move in the baptism service; they played down the work of the Holy Spirit. Thankfully, that sort of attitude is increasingly a thing of the past. Today there is widespread agreement that baptism is more than simply a rite or symbol.

Expect God to bless you

In many churches the laying on of hands now accompanies baptism. The leaders lay their hands on the person's head and pray, 'May God bless you and fill you with his Holy Spirit as you are baptised', or something like that. There is a definite anticipation that God will work in the life of the individual.

If you are about to be baptised, you need to be aware of what the Bible says about the individual's encounter with God in baptism (see Chapter 3), and you should have an expectation that you will encounter the Holy Spirit.

No one can do the work of God until he has the Holy Spirit and is endued with power.

G Campbell Morgan

Manifestations of the Spirit

I want to emphasise that baptism is a supernatural event. Getting into a pool of water is, of course, a physical act. But there is no question that God does honour people who come to their baptism ready to receive from him. So you should not treat your baptism simply as an act of obedience or a duty you have to perform, which will not make any actual difference to your life. I know many people who have experienced the working of the Holy Spirit while in the baptism pool. Some of those people have been very quiet and still, experiencing a great sense of peace; some have cried, some have laughed, some have shaken, some have spontaneously spoken in tongues. None of these activities of the Spirit is better or more holy than any other. He will do what he chooses.

I never tell people to expect a specific manifestation; I simply tell them that they will encounter God in their baptism. We never know how he will move: he works in the way he wants to work in each individual. He might impart one of the spiritual gifts to a person in the pool, or he might give them a healing emotional release or a simple sense of elation. In some cases the person will not feel any strong emotion at all at the time, but that does not mean that God has not met with him or her.

If you are preparing for baptism, I would like to encourage you to get excited about the encounter with God which will happen in the pool. You may receive spiritual gifts you have not had before, or gifts you already have may take on new dimensions. Even if there is no laying on of hands at the service, you will still encounter God in your baptism if you approach it with an expectant attitude.

When are we going to learn that all the wonderful things we read about in the book of Acts were simply the outflow and the overflow of the inflow of the Holy Spirit?

Vance Havner

Wait a minute!

There is no need to rush out of the pool once you have been baptised: it's a good idea to just stand there for a few moments, dripping wet. Wait in the water and sing your baptismal song, which you have chosen and which means so much to you. You will only ever be baptised once – enjoy it! Your baptism truly is the opportunity of a lifetime. Don't hurry out of God's presence. I believe that often God wants to bless people in the pool and to affirm that what they have done is right and to confirm their commitment to him, but often it's all over too fast. As soon as they are raised out of the water they rush out of the pool. So I often whisper in the person's ear as he or she stands up in the water again, 'Just wait a minute. Relax – enjoy God's presence'.

… the Holy Spirit will come upon you and give you power. Then you will tell everyone about me…

Acts 1:8

SANDIE: '... released from a fear of failure'

Sandie experienced the Holy Spirit's power in her baptism. She writes:

'I knew baptism was a step of obedience for me. My family had belonged to a denomination in which believer's baptism was not practised. My spiritual life had been stunted and I wanted very much to grow as a Christian and to receive more from God so that I could begin to be more effective in working out his purposes in my own life and in the world around me. My life had been characterised by fear and failure. I had been fearful during my childhood and teens because of an unhappy and chaotic home life. I felt a failure because I was used to everything going wrong. My first marriage failed, and at that point I became a Christian through meeting Des, my second husband, who has always encouraged and affirmed everything I try to do.

'One thing I asked the Lord to do for me during my baptism was to free me from fear and to help me leave it in the past. I wanted to be released into a new future, without the feeling of being a failure which had so dominated my life, and even my 11 years as a Christian.

'I remember writing my testimony at home over and over again, but when I stood up to read it out at the service I hardly needed to look down at the words, because God had given me a new confidence, even before I was actually baptised. I felt totally unafraid.

'I remember the love and prayers of God's worshipping people as I stepped into the water to be baptised. I felt total peace and joy as I went under the water. I felt washed and bathed in God's love as I came up out of the water. Then the Lord gave me these words through our associate minister: "You are a handmaiden of the Lord. Do not be afraid. Whatever I ask of you, do not be afraid." I was absolutely overjoyed by this and I began to sing with real meaning the words of "I just want to praise you", the song I had chosen for my baptism.

'God met me in the pool that day and began a healing process which is still going on four years later. Since then, whenever I have been challenged to do something for the Lord, instead of feeling frightened and sure that I would fail, I have remembered those words at my baptism. It's only when I'm not close enough to God that I become defeated again. I have certainly found that God can do "immeasurably more than we imagine".

'I believe that my baptism was an important key which unlocked a lot of pain that needed to be dealt with. Praise God that he wants us to be healed and victorious! I could write pages and pages about God's victory in my life since I was baptised: he has enabled me to witness effectively and to meet the challenge of being a house group leader; he has healed my attitude towards my relatives, my father in particular… '

DAVE: '… freed from a fear of death'

Here's the testimony of another Christian whose life was changed by the power of the Holy Spirit as a result of baptism:

'I had been a Christian for about six years when I began to think seriously about believer's baptism. One day I sat down and said to the Lord, "If you really want me to be baptised, give me the song you want sung at the service". Within seconds the words of the hymn, "Breathe on me, breath of God" filled my mind. My first reaction was, "Oh no! Why not something more modern?" But I knew it was right when I read the words of the hymn and discussed the matter with our pastor.

'Since becoming a Christian I had great doubts about my own personal salvation. I believed that my Christian friends and relations would go to be with the Lord, but for some reason I could never accept it for myself. In fact I had a real phobia about death.

I used to count the bathroom tiles (there were about 80) to work out the percentage of my life I had left. I never allowed myself to look forward to anything, because the passage of time simply meant I would be that much nearer to death. No amount of prayer or counselling helped.

'I didn't really want to be baptised because I dislike having water on my head, but I knew it was something I had to do. I was baptised, but I felt a bit disappointed because I didn't feel any different. It was about three weeks later that I realised that I no longer had a fear about death – in fact I had just not thought about it since my baptism. God had indeed breathed on me. That was 10 years ago, and the fear has never returned.'

To recap:

• Expect God to bless you in your baptism. It's a supernatural event!

• Don't rush out of the pool once you have been baptised: wait a moment and enjoy God 's presence.

9

Into the wilderness

A sense of elation is the usual immediate response to baptism. If you have prepared for it properly and you have approached it with expectancy, you will probably experience a 'high' afterwards, perhaps lasting for several days. You may feel on top of the world and want to do everything with a new enthusiasm. God will feel very real and close to you, and the problems which you have in your life will look very small and insignificant.

This feeling of euphoria is good and is something to thank God for. However, some people don't feel anything very special at the time of their baptism and get this sense of elation later.

A spiritual pattern

People who experience a 'high' after their baptism often find that a reaction sets in within a month. Over the years I have observed a pattern here, and it bears a strong resemblance to the experience of Jesus.

When Jesus was baptised, the Holy Spirit came upon him saying, 'You are my own dear Son, and I am pleased with you' (Luke 3:22). Afterwards John the Baptist said, 'Here is the Lamb of God who takes away the sin of the world! … I tell you that he is the Son of God' (John 1:29,34). For Jesus there must have been a tremendous sense of excitement, destiny and mission at the time of his baptism. There was a great feeling of drama there, down by the River Jordan.

But after all this Jesus was sent into the wilderness by the Holy Spirit and had to endure forty days and nights without food. In addition, he had to resist three powerful temptations from

Satan. Only after this time in the wilderness did his ministry proper begin.

Something similar seems to happen to Christians after their baptisms. I don't want to suggest that this is some kind of cast-iron theological principle, but the reaction happens so frequently that it is most definitely a spiritual pattern. Not everyone goes through a low period after baptism. If you don't, be thankful. But I believe that Jesus' experience after his baptism was included in the Bible partly to teach us what can happen to Christians at this crucial time.

Your enemy, the devil, is like a roaring lion, prowling around to find someone to attack.

1 Peter 5:8

Testing times

After a baptism service I write to the people I have baptised, telling them to thank God for the elation they probably feel, but also warning them that testing times may come. The devil is not pleased with the step of obedience they have taken in getting baptised, and they should expect to be attacked spiritually. It's a case of 'the bigger they are, the harder they fall' – their spiritual 'stature' has been increased by the public declaration of faith they have made, and the devil now tries all the harder to bring them down. They have more to lose than they had before. By being baptised they have clearly identified themselves as full-time, committed members of God's army, rather than. people who volunteer to help now and then when it suits them. Satan now knows that they are his enemies. Their baptism is a serious statement about their involvement in the spiritual war which is going on.

People often have a great feeling of security and certainty at their baptism and in the days following it: 'God is alive and here with me now; all is well with the world; God is here on planet Earth, and I love him and he loves me.' But suddenly this feeling disappears! It's like walking over a precipice – all those wonderful thoughts and emotions just evaporate.

The first step on the way to victory is to recognise the enemy.

Corrie ten Boom

This spiritual low following baptism is often worse than the low periods which people might have experienced previously. Maybe then they used to say to themselves, 'But everything will be all right once I've been baptised.' Now they have been baptised, and they are still experiencing doubts and despondency! People then think, 'This shouldn't be happening. It's all my fault – there must be something terribly wrong with me!'

Perhaps God allows us to be tested in this way to remind us that our walk with him is more than just a matter of temporary feelings – we must walk by faith and not by sight.

However, I should emphasise that while a low after the high of baptism is likely, it is not inevitable. I always tell the people I baptise not to deliberately look for such a reaction. I encourage them to focus on Jesus rather than look around every corner thinking, 'Maybe the devil's going to attack me!'

Biblical examples

There are plenty of stories in the Bible which clearly illustrate this pattern of tough times following spiritual blessings, and we can take strength and encouragement from these examples.

After his resounding victory over the prophets of Baal, Elijah experienced an acute case of spiritual depression. He sat down under a tree and prayed, 'I've had enough. Just let me die!' (1 Kings 19:4). But God lovingly restored his spiritual health.

John the Baptist had an amazingly powerful ministry, and publicly declared his faith that Jesus was 'the Lamb of God who takes away the sin of the world!' (John 1:29). And yet in his lonely prison cell he told his disciples to ask Jesus 'Are you the one we should be looking for? Or must we wait for someone else?' (Matthew 11:3).

The prophet Jonah was blessed with a commission from God to go and preach against the wicked city of Nineveh. But Jonah was so overwhelmed by this that he boarded a ship bound for a very distant place called Tarshish (Jonah 1:1–3). He felt he couldn't cope with what God had called him to do. He finally obeyed God and preached in Nineveh but, ironically, he was extremely fed up when the Ninevites listened to his message and repented!

One of the things which these stories show us is that God is always faithful to us, despite our emotional and spiritual ups and downs. Elijah, John the Baptist and Jonah felt that they had let God down and that he was far away, but in fact he was always with them.

False expectations

Sometimes people run into problems after their baptism because other people then have higher expectations of them. The people we live and work with may have seen us get baptised and make our declaration of faith, and so now they expect us to be completely holy at all times. Every time we lose our temper or swear or behave badly in any way, we feel that we are being watched and judged in a way that we weren't before baptism. So you should be ready for the possibility that other people's expectations of you will rise to unrealistic heights once you have been baptised.

Also, you should watch out for unrealistic expectations from yourself! You may think that now that you have been baptised you have 'arrived' spiritually. 'God has blessed me, and I feel great, and I'm ready to go out and convert the whole world!' In a sense you are on an artificial high: although God has indeed blessed you in your baptism, and you may have some new spiritual gifts, there is no question about the fact that the emotion of the moment cannot last. So although you will, hopefully, have been permanently transformed by your baptism, you cannot expect the warm, glowing feelings of the occasion to last forever. Sometimes Satan uses this to make us have new doubts about ourselves and our faith, and quite quickly we descend from the baptism day's absolute certainty to the misery of rock bottom, wondering 'Was it all a fake?' It's not unusual for people to think, a month or so after their baptism, 'Did I imagine it all? Was it really that wonderful? Where is God, now that all the fuss has died down?' It is important to battle through all that, because normally this period of doubt and despondency is temporary.

> We often suffer, but we are never crushed. Even when we don't know what to do, we never give up. In times of trouble, God is with us, and when we are knocked down, we get up again.
>
> 2 Corinthians 4:8,9

I find it remarkable that I have never read about this post-baptism phenomenon anywhere. Because of the lack of teaching on the subject, many people are quite unaware that baptism is often followed by a spiritual reaction. When people know that they may experience an attack, they are to some degree protected from its worst effects.

It is also important to remember that if you have done even half of the preparatory disciplines which I suggested in Chapters 5 and 6 – doing a discipleship course, seeing a spiritual director, reading the Bible and helpful Christian books, preparing your testimony, repenting, praying, fasting and so on – your attention will have been focused on your spiritual life, and this will have had very beneficial results. But if, after your baptism, you cease to do all these things, the euphoric feelings you had on the big day will, of course, tend to evaporate, because you will not be cultivating your spiritual life with the same intensity. We need to keep on practising these disciplines: they are necessary for our long-term spiritual health and not just for the period preceding baptism.

A four-stage attack

The devil's strategy after baptism is the same as his usual one: that is, he breaks down a Christian's faith first through disillusionment, then through despair, then through isolation and finally through rejection. This four-stage attack is particularly potent after baptism.

Disillusionment: Christians begin to feel disillusioned when they discover that the spiritual high of their baptism day was only a temporary experience. Those wonderful feelings of blessing – of God being so close, of God's love being almost tangible seem to have disappeared into thin air.

Despair: Disillusionment leads to despair. Post-baptism 'high', people begin to think, in the words of the old hymn, 'Where is the blessedness that once I knew when first I saw the Lord?' They start to dwell on their depressed state, and so they become caught in a downward spiral.

Isolation: Satan then makes a key move and gets them isolated, thinking thoughts like, 'Why is this happening to me? I must have sinned – I must have done something wrong. I'm not worthy to call myself a Christian. I must be the only person this has ever happened to. I must be either especially sinful or especially weak. Maybe God just doesn't love me. Maybe I just made up all that excitement I felt on my baptism day.' Believing they are some kind of spiritual misfit, and feeling ashamed and agonised and embarrassed about it, they are unwilling to seek help.

Rejection: Then comes rejection. These Christians feel rejected by God, and so they reject God and his Church. They think, 'Why is God allowing me to suffer in this way? It must be because he doesn't love me. So why should I bother to worship him or be committed to him? And as for all these other Christians, they don't seem to know or care about what I'm going through. And even if they did know, they wouldn't understand – they're far too spiritual and holy! They don't care about me – so why should I have anything to do with them?'

> If God is on our side, can anyone be against us? ... In everything we have won more than a victory because of Christ who loves us.
>
> Romans 8:31,37

Don't give in!

The enemy may attack us after baptism, but we don't have to give in to it. We don't have to lie down and let him walk all over us! In the next chapter I will explain how a Christian can stay out of the downward spiral and so prevent disillusionment from developing into despair.

DIANA: 'The enemy is very subtle.'

Diana's experience of baptism illustrates the points I have made in this chapter. She encountered some problems both during her baptism service and afterwards. She writes:

'As I read out my testimony and recalled all the events which had led up to my turning back to God... I started to shake uncontrollably. It was totally unexpected. I was thankful I had notes to read from, because I was experiencing great difficulty in stopping myself breaking down completely.

'Reading from my notes, I said, "That was the turning-point for me – that was when I turned back to God." I'm afraid that seems rather business-like, but I wanted it to sound like that, because I was trying to impress my very business-like non-Christian husband sitting in the front row. Also, I didn't want to let down my son by being over-emotional.

'I have to admit that the negative attitudes of my family – all except my son – to my baptism have stopped me recalling the joyful side of the event until now. The enemy is very subtle. I'm glad I've had this opportunity to put pen to paper and clarify my thoughts about it all.

'The first two weeks after my baptism were not very happy ones. Steve had written to me, warning me that I might experience an attack, and I did. But I praise the Lord that I answered his call to be baptised and am now walking in his light.'

To recap:

• Most people feel elated after their baptisms, but often a reaction sets in within a month or so.

• After your baptism, other people may have higher expectations of you.

• Also, you will probably have unrealistic expectations of yourself.

• Beware the devil's strategy: (1) disillusionment, (2) despair, (3) isolation and (4) rejection.

10

Winning moves

We have seen how the devil often attacks people after their baptisms with a four-stage strategy. But we can fight back and win with a strategic counter-attack.

A three-pronged counter-attack

1. Keep on doing the simple things well. Keep on praying, reading the Bible and having fellowship with other Christians – even though you are tempted to give up these things.

When you're driving your car and a fog comes down, all you can see is the Catseyes in the middle of the road. There is a temptation then to let your fear overwhelm you and just stop. But in fact you will be perfectly safe if you just carry on driving slowly and carefully to the left of the Catseyes. Similarly, if you are in a spiritual 'fog' or low you need to keep moving, guided by the little that you 'see' – that is, the familiar, regular aspects of your faith.

> The Devil cannot lord it over those who are servants of God with their whole heart and who place their hope in Him. The Devil will wrestle with, but not overcome them.
>
> The Shepherd of Hermas

It's a matter of trusting God. There is a game in which someone is blindfolded and they have to walk across a room without tripping or knocking anything over. Of course, the person can only do so with guidance, and someone else calling out precise instructions: 'Left a bit, forward one step, right a bit,' and so on. The blindfolded person can only get across the room if he or she trusts the guidance of the one calling out the directions. It's like this sometimes in the Christian life. Sometimes you can't see where you're going and you don't feel that God is with you, but if you do what you know to be right, following the instructions which, objectively, you know to be true (God's Word), sooner or later the ritual blindfold will slip off and you will be able to see clearly. To use a sporting analogy, when Steve Davis was deposed as top snooker player in the UK by Steven Hendry, Davis said, 'I just can't understand it – my whole game has fallen apart.' But afterwards he made a recovery and even beat Hendry a few times. Asked to account for his comeback, he said, 'I just went back to practising the things I learned when I first started playing this game. It had all become too complex. Now I have finally come out of the woods and I'm playing good snooker again.' He had learned the importance of doing the simple things well.

I think this is a message which needs to be emphasised to many of today's Christians: Don't neglect the basics of the faith!

> The best way to drive out the devil, if he will not yield to texts of Scripture, is to jeer and flout him, for he cannot bear scorn.
>
> Martin Luther

65

2. Share your feelings with someone in leadership. Sometimes doubts and disillusionment can be effectively dispelled by the prayers of someone in spiritual authority. If you go to a leader with your problem you will not feel isolated, because the leader will be able to assure you that you are not alone and that such feelings are common.

Don't be afraid to ask for help. Don't think that your leaders won't understand what it's like to have a problem. All Christians experience difficulties at times, and leaders are no exception. If you talk to them, you may discover that they are actually quite human!

3. Remember that this spiritual low won't last for ever. This experience is quite normal – even Jesus went through it. He eventually came out of the wilderness, and you will too. Don 't think that you will never again feel as you felt on your baptism day – you will! The realisation that the low will not last should prevent you from giving up hope.

After all, if you get toothache but you make an appointment with the dentist for later that day, you can put up with the discomfort, with the aid of something from the medicine cabinet, because you know that it won' t last. It would be a very different situation if you were told that the toothache was incurable and that you had to tolerate it permanently!

Spiritual time-lag

Another thing to bear in mind if you are suffering a spiritual reaction after baptism is that there is often a time-lag involved: it takes our feelings some time to catch up with the facts. We experience a rush of positive emotions at baptism, because it's such an exciting day, but it takes a while for all the blessings of our baptism to find their expression in our normal, daily feelings. So to begin with we may not feel any different after our baptism to how we felt before, and so we feel disappointed. The excitement of the day itself fades, and we are back to normal life. We may feel numb or empty and we may think, 'What an anticlimax!'

An antibiotic, not a pain-killer

Something many Christians need to understand is that baptism (like any blessing we receive from God) is more like an antibiotic than a pain-killer. The label on a bottle of antibiotics reads, 'Finish the course'. If you take some aspirin or paracetamol, the drug will quickly relieve your headache. But when you take antibiotics to cure an infection, for the first day or so you won't notice much difference in your health. In order to get some improvement you have to keep on taking the pills, and if you want to be completely well you have to finish the whole course or else the infection will return.

A similar principle applies in the Christian life. You have to take the 'medicine' for quite a while before you see any improvement in your spiritual 'health', and if you want to stay healthy you need to keep on taking the medicine.

'Did you really mean it?'

It's important to think of this difficult time after baptism as a time of testing. The seriousness of the oath of allegiance to Jesus which you have made by being baptised is being tested. God is asking you, 'Did you really mean it?' Are you really committed to him or are you just a seven-day wonder? Are you going to grit your teeth through this testing time or are you going to give up, now that the euphoria of your baptism day has evaporated? Are you going to trust God, or are you going to let your feelings rule you? Feelings do tend to play a large part in the experience of young Christians, but as they mature they are asked increasingly to walk not by sight (that is, feelings) but by faith.

> He who with his whole heart draws near unto God must of necessity be proved by temptation and trial.

> Albert the Great

This principle is perfectly compatible with natural human development. Children have a far greater capacity for excitement than adults, because everything is new to them. Adults' feelings are not as swiftly stimulated as children's. I could make my young daughters jump up and down and shriek with excitement quite easily, just by promising to take them to the zoo. What would someone have to say to me to make me very excited? It would have to be something more than an offer to take me to see some elephants and gorillas!

As we mature, our emotions become more settled. We become less dependent upon our feelings. The same thing is true of our spiritual development as Christians. God wants us to depend less on our feelings and more on his Spirit, his will and his Word. We ought to begin to learn this lesson in the period after baptism.

Learning to hang in there

So after baptism there is much to learn about perseverance and tenacity in our faith. Our motto should be 'When the going gets tough, the tough get going'. Of course, this sort of discipline is completely against the trend of the society in which we live. People aren't used to the idea of persevering with something.

When they were quite young my children were members of a gymnastics club for a while. Then they wanted to join a different club … and after that something else. I suppose that sort of 'flightiness' is not unusual in children. But today a lot of adults are like that too. It is very rarely the case that someone is a lifelong member of a club. Men used to support the same football club for 50 years! That sort of thing happens far less often today, partly due to the greater mobility of our society. There must be tens of thousands of Manchester United supporters all over the· country – and around the world – who have never in their lives been to the Old Trafford stadium!

Great works are performed not by strength but by perseverance.

Samuel Johnson

Today people's allegiances and affections are much more loose and changeable than they used to be. In previous generations many churches had a rule that someone had to be a member for five years before they could be in leadership. If churches kept that rule today they might never have any leaders, because people often move on within five years.

We live in a society in which transience is the order of the day. I'm old enough to remember the first appearance of the Rubik's Cube. In the 1980s this was an extremely popular toy for both adults and children. Everybody had one! But, despite a recent attempt to revive it, it was a passing fad, and there are probably thousands of Rubik's Cubes forgotten about in cupboards and attics, along with many other five-minute wonders.

Sad to say, some people treat their Christian faith that way: it's on a shelf, gathering dust. Their attitude is, 'Christianity was a phase I went through, but I grew out of it.'

Also, it's true that people have much more choice about religion than generations ago. Today the shelves of the religious 'supermarket' are crammed. You can buy into absolutely any belief you wish. Or any combination of beliefs. It's even OK to invent your own! Once Christianity was more or less the only 'product' on offer. Some people alter their religious allegiance in much the same way as they change their brand of washing powder.

So anyone who perseveres as a Christian is swimming against the flow of our modern western culture, in which things like loyalty and tenacity are alien concepts. If we are to be disciples of Jesus we must have a permanent commitment to him and a determination to persevere in our faith, no matter what happens. We need to hang in there, to stick at it. Many of those who fall by the wayside after baptism do so because they have not really understood this need for perseverance. They think that the Christian life is going to be easy, and when they discover it's not, they give up.

While on the one hand it's true that we must be totally committed to God, on the other hand it's also crucial to remember that God is totally committed to us. It's not all up to us! He has said, 'The Lord has promised that he will not leave us or desert us' (Hebrews 13:5). The apostle Paul declared confidently that 'God is the one who began this good work in you, and I am certain that he won't stop before it is complete on the day that Christ Jesus returns' (Philippians 1:6).

To recap:

How to fight back against a spiritual low:

• Keep on doing the simple things well.

• Share your feelings with someone in leadership.

• Remember that this spiritual low won't last for ever.

• There's often a spiritual time-lag: it takes our feelings some time to catch up with the facts.

• Remember – the Christian faith is more like an antibiotic than a pain-killer.

• The period after baptism is often a time when your commitment to Jesus Christ is tested.

• As we mature, God wants us to depend less on our feelings and more on his Spirit, his will and his Word.

• As we mature, we need to learn about perseverance in our faith.

11

Only the beginning

In chapters 9 and 10 we looked at the sorts of things which we can expect to happen in the period immediately following baptism. In this chapter I want to talk about the Christian's long-term experience after baptism – about his or her life as a disciple of Jesus Christ.

Departure not destination

Sometimes people see baptism as a kind of destination. That's understandable, because there's a great deal of work involved in it, if you prepare for it properly. It's like going on holiday. After weeks of careful planning, you step off the train or plane at your destination. You've arrived!

But in fact baptism is not arriving – it is getting on the train at the start of your journey, the journey that's your Christian life. Baptism is a point of departure and not a destination.

Church membership

In the Bible, baptism and church membership are very closely linked. When you are baptised into Christ you are also baptised into his Body, the Church. By being baptised you are identifying yourself not only with Christ but also with the Church, and moreover, with a particular local church. Whatever part of the Body you may be – a toe, a finger, a nose, an eye – you have a function and a role to play within the Body. It is quite inappropriate to think of yourself as a lone ranger.

By being baptised you have become a member of God 's army. You can't operate by yourself – you have to stand alongside the other soldiers. Being a member of that army implies commitment not just to the commanding officer but also to the army as a whole. Baptism and membership of the Church ought to be thought of as two sides of the same coin.

Unfortunately, the local church is often an afterthought for those who get baptised. This is symptomatic of the individualism of our age. We are excessively concerned about 'what I want', and 'what I should do' and 'how I should live my Christian life'. Innumerable Christian books have been written about me feeling fulfilled and me having answers to my prayers and me discovering my gifts and my ministry and so on. I think we have to a great extent lose the corporate dimension of the Christian life which the Bible emphasises so strongly.

The fact that we are baptised not only into the name of Jesus but also into his Body means that we have to take the Church seriously, despite all its faults. Your local church is not perfect – in fact, it may have a whole host of problems. The leaders may seem inadequate, the sermons dull, the structure inappropriate, there may not be enough activities for teenagers and young marrieds, and so on. But you are called to be a member of your local church, because that is part of what baptism is about. Church membership is a very important part of your life as a Christian. It should keep you strong and secure in your faith, keep you growing, and make you an effective soldier in God's army – a fellow traveller rather than a mere passenger.

Witnessing

The excitement you feel about being baptised should lead you to tell other Christians about the blessings of baptism. There will always be those around who are on the Christian journey but who have not yet sensed the importance of believer's baptism. You can be a willing advocate of baptism to those people. You can tell them what God has done for you, and that will stimulate them into obedience and into receiving all the blessings that come through baptism. This is an area of witness which is usually overlooked, because we think of witnessing as something we do only to non-Christians.

Of course, our baptism can also be a witness to non-Christians. Witnessing to them keeps us looking outwards and makes us objective in our understanding of the faith instead of introspective. This is always the danger for us: that we will become focused on our own personal faith. It's so important to look outwards and tell others, especially non-Christians, about what God has done for us.

Both my parents were teachers. They used to say that they only ever got sick in the holidays, because during term time they were so busy that they didn't have time to be ill! While their attention was focused on their work, they were healthy, but when the term ended they had time to think about themselves, and then it was easy to notice how tired they felt and to catch a cold.

When Christians stop looking outwards to others we focus on ourselves too much and this makes all the problems we have seem bigger, breeding doubt and tension. So an outward focus after baptism is very important – we need to look out to those who don't know and love the Lord.

Crisis and process

Baptism is a crisis – a one-off, never-to-be-repeated experience. But spirituality – our Christian journey – is a process of growth. We need to go on being filled with the Holy Spirit day by day; we need to go on discovering our spiritual gifts; we need to be persistent in prayer; we need to go on asking, seeking and knocking (Matthew 7:7); we need to keep on asking to be filled with the love of God, so that we can give his love to others. We need to go on practising the basic spiritual disciplines: prayer, the reading of scripture and fellowship with other Christians. These things are an essential part of our preparation for baptism, but they are also crucial to our long-term growth as Christians.

So, baptism is the departure-point for our journey with Christ; only the start of the process of spiritual growth. We have to go on growing. As Christians we have options: going forwards or going backwards. We cannot stand still. We live in a stream which is flowing against us, so as soon as we stop trying to move forwards, we will drift backwards.

Soldiers in God's army

Generally speaking, God does not use ideologies or governments to achieve his purposes: he uses individuals. God's tools for changing the world are people. I feel strongly that at the beginning of a new century we need a whole army of people with a tremendous sense of call on their lives, with a desire to do something of eternal significance rather than get involved in the trivialities of this generation, which is so obsessed with materialism, leisure and pleasure.

The presence of the Holy Spirit endues people with divine authority and power. He does not work through organisations but through people.

Samuel Chadwick

The preacher CT Studd once remarked that, compared with the Christians of yesterday, the Christians of today are 'chocolate soldiers': we melt when things get hot and we break under the slightest pressure. We are wimps! We need to change – to become determined, battle-hardened warriors for Christ.

If you have been baptised, you have put on your spiritual armour, and you are ready for battle. If you have not yet been baptised, then don't miss out on the special blessings which baptism brings. Baptism is part of the equipment which God wants to give us to enable us to serve him.

Christians are soldiers in God's army, and we have a war to fight. We must go out into God's world and win it back for him. Missionary pioneer William Carey said, 'Expect great things of God; attempt great things for God.' That should be our motto. Let's be people who make a real difference to the world in this generation – let's make the Kingdom of God a reality in our society.

My most cherished possession I wish I could leave you is my faith in Jesus Christ. For with Him and nothing else you can be happy, but without Him and with all else you'll never be happy.

Patrick Henry

To recap:

• Baptism is a point of departure – not a destination.

• When you are baptised into Christ you are also baptised into his Body, the Church.

• You are excited about your baptism, so tell other people about it – Christians and non-Christians.

• Baptism is a one-off event, but spirituality is a process.

• Now that you have been baptised, get involved in the battle!

Preparing for your baptism – seven days with God through Bible reading and prayer

The Bible is alive because it is a major way that God himself chooses to communicate with us. Often when we read it the words leap off the page and speak to us personally. The Bible is a power that can literally change lives.

And the Bible is a handbook or manual for life. Although it doesn't have an exact answer for every specific question, through reading it we begin to understand God 's perspective, which will inform our choices, attitudes, lifestyle.

Plan to spend time with God and his Word as part of your preparation for baptism. Here is a seven-day reading plan to use.

A pattern for reading

Come to the Bible expectantly. Ask God through his Holy Spirit to give you understanding and a responsive heart and will. Read the verses carefully, listening for what God might want to say to you. Think about the meaning of the verses. Is God showing you anything about yourself or your life?

When you have finished reading, consider what might be an appropriate response. Prayer? Worship? Making a decision? Taking a particular action? A change in your attitude?

DAY 1 Confession l John 1:5–10

Take a few minutes to think about these verses. One aspect of baptism is a spiritual washing – getting ourselves clean. Say sorry to God about anything he shows you which needs to be put right.

DAY 2 A fresh start John 3:5–16 and Romans 6:4

Baptism is about dying to the old way of life and starting again with a new life and a new lifestyle. After thinking about these verses, ask God what differences there should be in your new, born-again life.

DAY 3 Membership 1 Corinthians 12:12–31

Baptism is about joining us to the Church, as well as to Christ. Pray for wisdom to discover what gifts God wants to release in you and what part he wants you to play in your local church.

DAY 4 Love 1 Corinthians 13:1–13

We get baptised not just because it's right, but as an expression of our love for God. This love for God must be extended to others. Pray that your baptism in water will also be a baptism in love.

DAY 5 Power Matthew 3:11–17

Baptism is a chance for an encounter with God. He wants to meet you in your baptism in a personal and powerful way. It's unlikely that a dove will appear, but don't let that put you off receiving all that God has for you!

DAY 6 Peace Philippians 4:4–9

It's easy to be anxious about being baptised. These verses should help! Pray that you will know God 's peace, now and in the months to come.

DAY 7 The future Hebrews 13:8 and Jude 24,25

Baptism is the beginning of your journey, not your destination! You won't be perfect until you get to heaven. Pray that you will be useful in God's service throughout your journey through life.

Also available from Faithbuilders

First Steps A down-to-earth explanation of how to live when you make a decision to follow Christ. No heavy theology, but a practical, light approach with plenty of humour. Sound biblical teaching with street cred. Warm, positive and relevant to today's world; an ideal book for new believers, post-Alpha and enquirers groups.

It Makes Sense Best-selling humorous and compelling look at the reasons it makes sense to be a Christian. Covers science, suffering, other faiths, and many other issues.

BV - #0031 - 070622 - C0 - 229/152/5 - PB - 9781912120413 - Matt Lamination